Griggs International Academy (Griggs) is the online school for the North American Division of Seventh-Day Adventists. We are proud to be one of the oldest distance-education schools around! Long before computers existed, the children of missionary families would do their school work, send their lessons by boat to "Fireside Correspondence School" where they were marked by a teacher and then sent, by boat, back to the student. We have come a long way since 1909!! We are proudly on the campus of Andrews University where we interact with thousands of students in almost 60 countries every day!

One of our favorite areas of growth has been in developing personal relationships between staff, students, and teachers. The times we get to spend together collaborating on projects and finding ways to engage has been so rewarding. The book you are holding is the result of some of those relationships and collaborations. We are excited to share with you some of the ways God has impacted our lives. As stated in our mission:

Griggs International Academy seeks to
INSPIRE learning,
TRANSFORM lives
and SERVE the world
through Seventh-day Adventist Christian education.

We hope you will be Inspired, Transformed, and Served well as you read, journal and doodle in these pages.

Our challenge to you is to spend the next weeks pondering the verses and stories shared here, and journaling about how they have impacted and encouraged you.

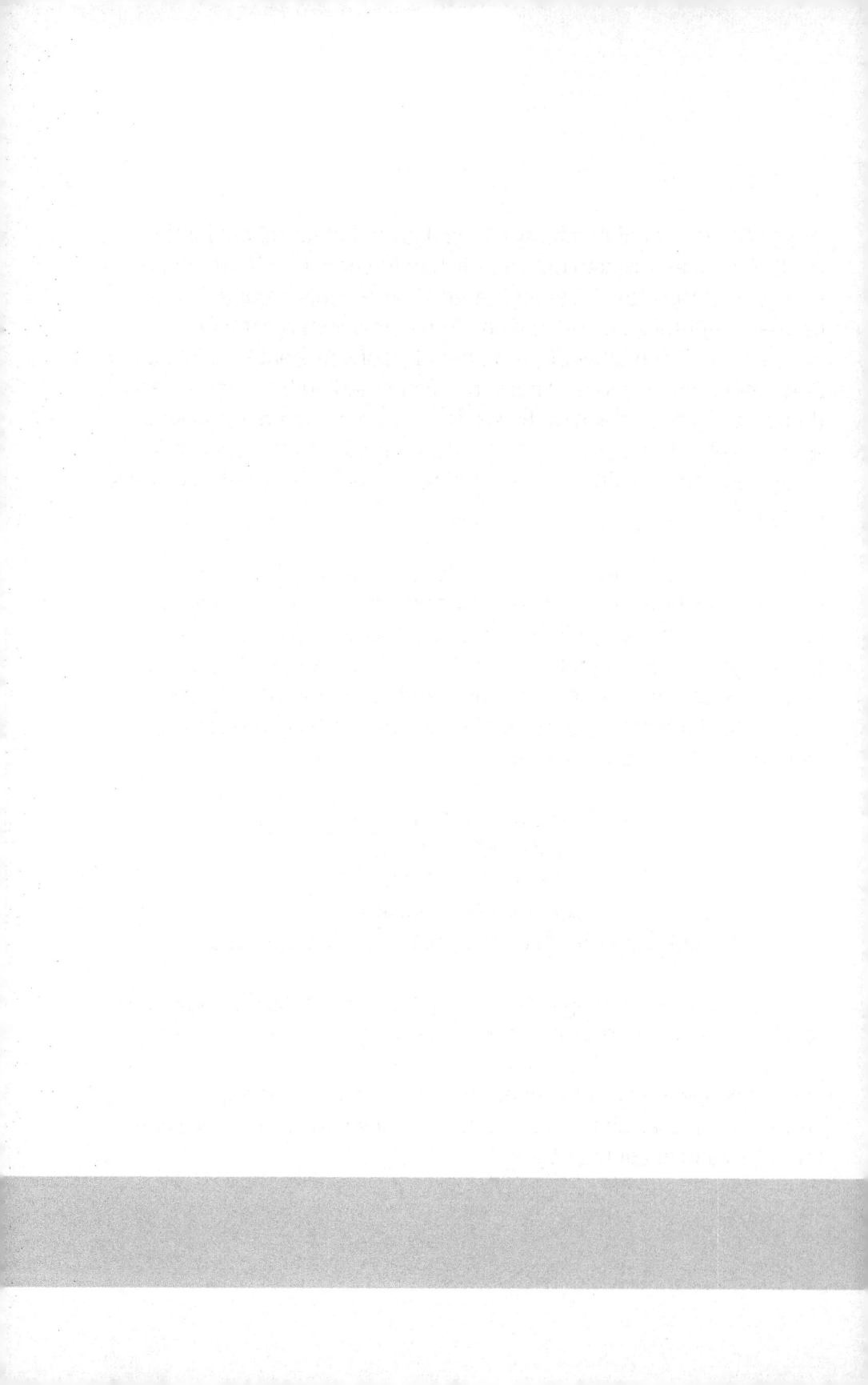

The following students and staff of Griggs International Academy are contributors to this collection of devotional thoughts:

Abram Motlhaapula
Aleeiah Hettel
Amy Alejandra Trejos Velosa
Anastasia Markovic
Ashley Shultz
Avianna Codner
Ben Kreiter
Britoya Thomas
Divini-Loryn Belle
Elsa Balint
Evans Jr Tawananyasha Muvuti
Finidy Rakotonarivelo
Harley Peterson

Jadon Kelly
Jessica Kovach
Lamar Nangle
La Ronda Forsey
Luz Gutierrez
Michaela Chapple
Morgan Wood
Nohelani James
Shane Witz
Shayla Robinson
Stephanie Goddard
Tammy Becker
Yuliya Hinckley

Design, doodles, and edits by Deirdré Korff Wilkens, Griggs Course Manager (@SewDoodleDe).

_____

_____

_____

_____

_____

_____

_____

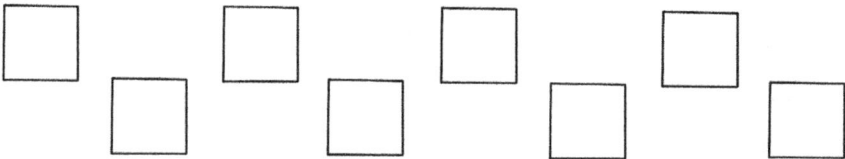

When we serve those around us, we serve God too.

God is not unjust; he will not forget your work and the love you have shown him as you have helped his people and continue to help them. Hebrews 6:10

Music is a very big part of my life. For as long as I can remember, I have always loved music. There is an activity that my friend group does once every three months. We go to the pediatric department in the hospital and bring things for the patients and their guardians. We bring snacks such as little juice boxes with fruit or a small packet of crisps. We read them Bible stories or funny stories that we prepared for them. We also share music with them by singing and/or playing our instruments. This really opened my eyes to how actions can be more powerful than words. The mothers appreciated our efforts and the little smiles we got from those kids were truly heart-warming. We did this before COVID-19 and wanted to do it again, but we are still trying to be cautious. It is really an event that brings joy to all those involved. We have to find a different way of sharing our little joys with them during Covid. We can't go visit them, but we can drop off little packets of snacks or baked goods and little messages of encouragement. We have even begun to include some younger kids, the older Adventurers, in helping us prepare these care packages. The older kids, my friends and I, buy the things such as snacks and the younger kids make cards and decorate them. We are hoping to show the younger kids that there are ways they can help others around them even with little things to do. Serving others doesn't have to be as big of an effort as we have done. Even little things like saying hello to someone you meet or even smiling to others can bring a little joy into that person's day.

Finidy R.   **Grade 10**

Nothing new under the sun, but what matters most is what's happening in Heaven.

The Lord wraps himself in light as with a garment; he stretches out the heavens like a tent.   Psalm 104:2 NIV

"There is no new thing under the sun" (Eccl 1:9) according to the wisest man on Earth, King Solomon, who penned these words between 930 and 970 BC. Yet it doesn't seem to stop generation after generation in the millennial years later from trying to invent, impress, and outdo one another.

A prime example would be a fashion show. It's rather difficult to be revolutionary when we've practically seen it all, and anything the brain and eye can imagine has strutted down the catwalk. Starting with conventional materials: silk, cotton, linen, polyester, leather, velvet, etc. Recycled: trash bags, potato chip bags, caution tape, newspapers, egg cartons, and bubble wrap. Food: raw beef or chocolate. Odd and precarious: acrylics, ropes, silicone, feathers, oil cloth, screen prints, and epoxy resins. The effect of these shows is to set a mood board and serve as a muse for the upcoming new fashion season, and to influence future trends and set themes.

Do you want to know a fashion that only comes from Heaven? In Psalms 104:2 we learn that God wraps light around Him like a garment. This light clung to Moses after his time on the mountain with the Lord (Ex 34:29) and Jesus was covered in dazzling light as He was transfigured back to Heaven (Mark 9:2,3). Matthew witnessed that the angel who rolled away the stone from Jesus' tomb appeared as a fiery white light (28:3).

One day in Heaven we will be wearing Heaven-made garments, but like Moses, God's glory will shine around us. I like to imagine that we will never be hot or cold because we will be basking in God's warmth like the rays of the earthly sun warming us now.

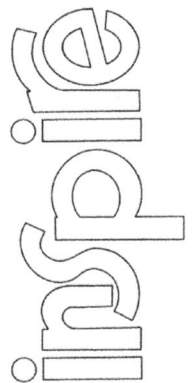

inspire

Stephanie G.   **Teacher**

He replied, "Whether he is a sinner or not, I don't know. One thing I do know. I was blind but now I see!"   John 9:25 NIV

Fifteen miles of hiking, a rainy weekend, and no running water: three ingredients to equal a fun but exhausting camping weekend. My husband and I had traveled up to the beautiful Upper Peninsula of Michigan to camp at Pictured Rocks National Lakeshore with our friends, Nicole & Andrew. As we packed up the tent in the pattering rain, we laughed at how dirty we all looked from the adventure. A short two hour drive brought us to our homebase for the rest of the week: a little cabin on the edge of a lake.

How welcoming the rustic cabin felt! While the rooms were tiny and air conditioning wasn't to be found, compared to the tent we had shared the previous two nights as rain kept us awake, we were living in luxury! As the afternoon light started to change into a warmer hue, we cooked a simple supper and enjoyed it on the patio.

Everything seemed perfect until we heard a shriek from inside the cabin! "A mouse!" Nicole yelled, " I think I saw a mouse!" A conversation ensued where we wondered if it really happened or if it had only been a shadow. We went to bed a little uneasy but hoped perhaps it had all been an illusion.

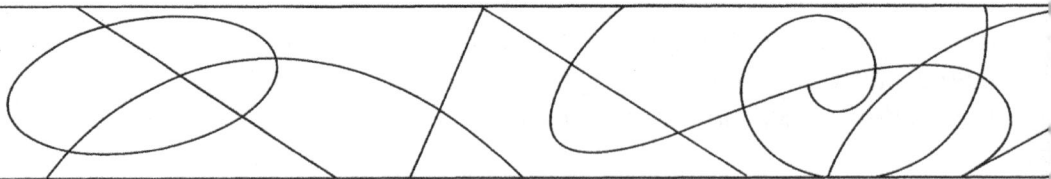

Take a moment to think about a change in perspective or life you've experienced in your life recently. How do you see God's presence as you work through the effects of that transformation?

The next morning dawned clear as we started on pancakes for breakfast. While we were in the middle of preparing the food, who should appear but a small, furry mouse! The mouse from last night indeed was real!

Throughout the rest of our trip, the little rodent would appear 3-5 times each day. We tried to catch him in a homemade trap so he would leave us alone. Food was moved into our car and we stomped around a little more than usual when walking past the various holes the most often appeared. Our cozy cabin wasn't as charming as before.

There are moments or events in life that can change your perspective in an instant. We might even wish that we could go back to how we felt or saw the world before, but undoing that moment of transformation is impossible. Like our cabin experience, the only thing left to do is to take a deep breath and embrace the change we now see. And to know that whatever the experience, God is there to be our strength - and sometimes laugh with us!

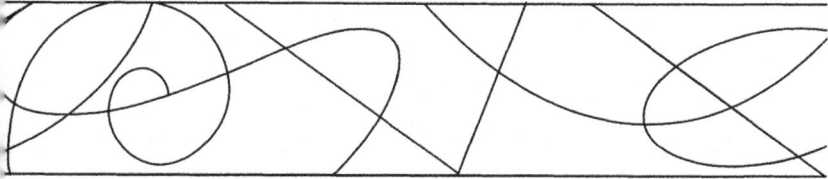

Jessica K.   **Staff**

While I had been signing since I was 11 years old, I did not really know how to interpret from English to American Sign Language (or vice versa) until I was older. I knew God called me to be an ASL interpreter when I was young, but it was after I became an Adventist that I knew God wanted me to be an interpreter for the Seventh-day Adventist Church. As a teenager, I attended the Sacramento Central SDA Church in Sacramento, California. At the time when I was there, Pastor Doug Batchelor was my pastor; both he and his wife became my friends. When I was old enough, I enrolled in the community college in Sacramento and started taking ASL Classes to work towards my interpreting degree. Eventually I was able to enroll into the Interpreter Training Program.

It was Fall 1999 and I had just started learning how to interpret, but I was not proficient yet. Sacramento Central was doing a Fall Evangelistic program at the church and Pastor Doug called me to ask if I would be willing to interpret the meetings into ASL. I was scared to death and told him, "Pastor Doug, I cannot interpret yet!" His words to me were, "Well, we had a meeting about the evangelist program and we want to offer this to the Deaf community. I view it as getting your feet wet - you can try it and see how it goes." I reluctantly agreed. I knew the first night when the words from Revelation started being preached that I was in way over my

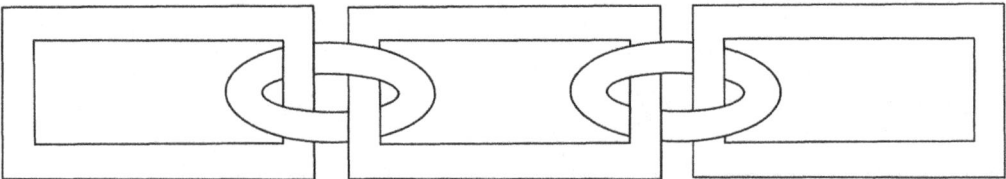

If you are willing, God can use you to serve Him

head. I had no idea how to sign these symbols, much less interpret them! Thankfully, I had no Deaf in attendance. I was discouraged, but felt that I must continue because I gave my word. It was on the third night of the meeting that a Deaf woman came to the meetings and was thrilled that I was there. No, I had not met her before, but she was so touched that I was willing to muddle through the interpreting that she cried. Nancy, my new Deaf friend, had been praying that God would lead her to the right place to meet an Adventist interpreter. God led her to the meetings at Sacramento Central Church and met me there. She and her husband became some of my dearest friends. Did I interpret those meetings efficiently? Nope, not at all. God did something else; He used me to touch another life and prove to her that He was listening to her prayers. That was a tremendous blessing.

God used me to serve in a few ways; first, I was willing to be used by God to serve another person the very best that I could with a basic ASL background. More than that, God used me to serve a purpose for someone else - that He still answers prayers.

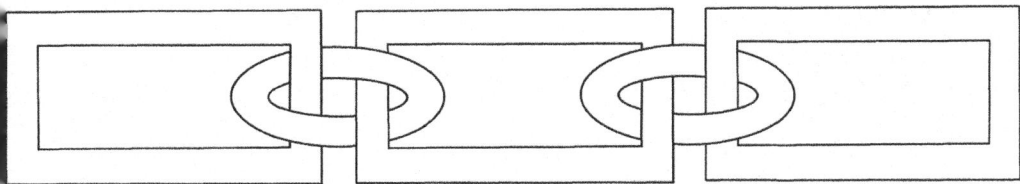

Nohelani J.   **Teacher**

_____

_____

_____

_____

_____

_____

_____

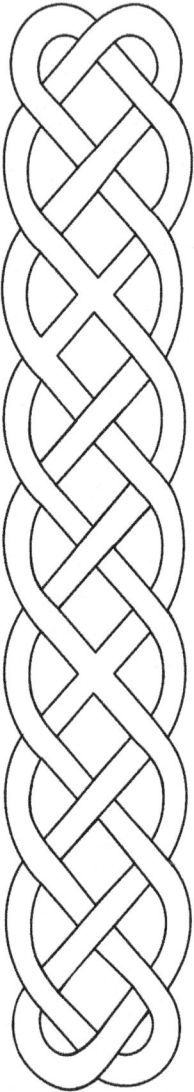

Through all things we must have a good mindset so that we may be able to show the love of Christ through all points in life

Finally, brethren, whatever things are true, whatever things are noble, whatever things are just, whatever things are pure, whatever things are lovely, whatever things are of good report, if there is any virtue and if there is anything praiseworthy—meditate on these things.   Philippians 4:8 NKJV

Do you ever find it hard to be positive? With the world that we live in, there are many ways that the enemy tries to bring us down in small ways such as doing badly on a test, getting sick, people bullying you, and the worst of them all, being unkind to yourself. I had this very same problem, and I constantly found myself unhappy. When I was negative and down, it was very hard to have a close relationship with God because I was so distracted.

I was transformed by having someone in my life being consistently positive and kind to everyone around them. I realized that with the negative attitude, I was missing great opportunities that could have been achieved if I had a positive one. Instead of falling into Satan's trap, we must pull closer to the Lord and use the Bible to give us inspiration. As John 16:33 states, " These things I have spoken to you, that in Me you may have peace. In the world you will have tribulation; but be of good cheer, I have overcome the world."

With this amazing knowledge we can transform the way we think and be kind for not only ourselves but for the people around us, and you will be shocked by the change God will make in your life!

Britoya T.   **Grade 11**

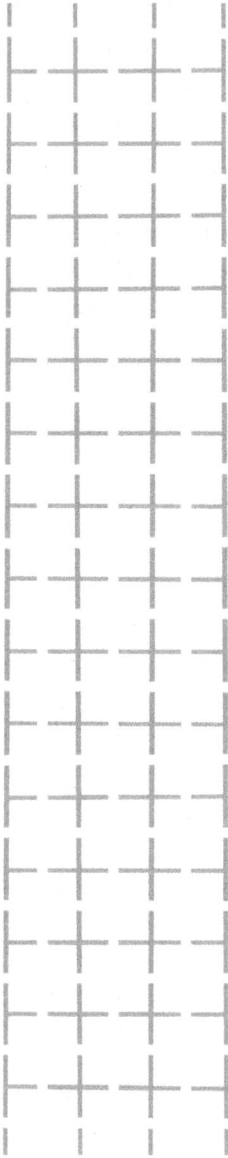

Look out for others around you because we all one in the family of God

Not looking to your own interests but each of you to the interests of the others. Philippians 2:4 NIV

The ten minute walk from my place to mma Ineeleng's house was custom to me, and always a delight. I would walk humming a song, and I could feel a special connection between me and the 88 year old lady.

Mma Ineeleng's health condition reached a point where she could not attend church worship as she used to; she had breathing difficulties, and she was also unable to stand on her feet for a long time. Serving mma Ineeleng by writing her tithe envelope, counting her money, and blessing the offerings meant a lot to me. I could feel the Holy Spirit hovering in that room. Her prayers were sincere and I learned how to pray earnestly. I understood the power of prayer by serving mma Ineeleng.

Among other errands, I would update her on the announcements from our local church. Her comments after listening attentively used to thrill me and made me realize that mma Ineeleng still understood the church organizational structure, and knew her rights as a baptized member of the Seventh-day Adventist Church.

The retired Literature Evangelist is now waiting for that glorious morning. It is my prayer that I keep the spirit of serving and be there for those who are in need of spiritual help. Prayer used to be our parting statements. It is these particular prayers that I learned and realized that distance does not matter, but it is assurance of safety that leads us to pray.

It hurts to see the elderly or disabled who aren't physically able to take themselves to church so I bring the church to them.

Abram M.   **Grade 11**

_____

_____

_____

_____

_____

_____

_____

_____

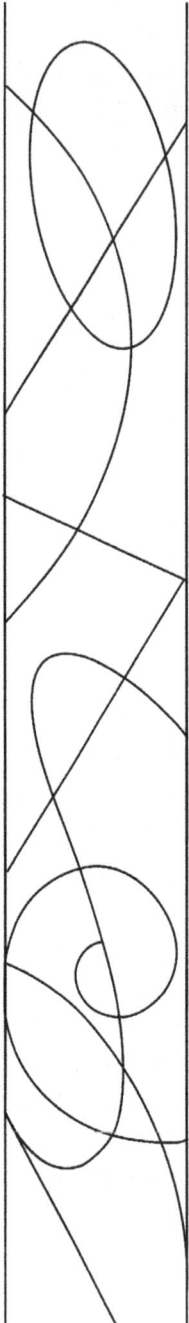

God calls you today, he wants you to put everything aside for a moment and spend some time learning from him and listening to his voice. God longs to transform your life.

I rise before the dawning of the morning, and cry for help; I hope in Your word... That I may meditate on Your word.

Psalm 119:147, 148

One of the most important things in a Christian's life is the time of the day when he connects with his creator to spend some time alone. Ever since I was little, my parents inspired me to make personal devotion an essential part of my life. I observed how they practiced daily devotions, and I was filled with emotion when they came to teach me how to do it on my own. As I got older, I began to understand and experience for myself the value of disconnecting from the world for a moment and taking time to praise God with songs, to study His word in depth, and to talk to him like a friend who is by my side ready to listen. Sometimes it is difficult because this world presents us with many challenges, where the hours of the day are not enough for everything we have to do, or we feel discouraged by so many problems. But devotionals can be that moment of peace in the midst of the storm, and I have seen how it has transformed my life to the point that when I don't do it, I feel empty or incomplete. God calls you today, he wants you to put everything aside for a moment and spend some time learning from him and listening to his voice. God longs to transform your life.

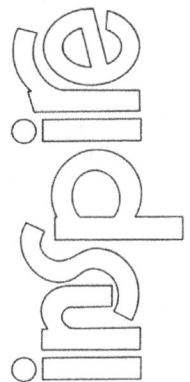

inspire

Amy V.   **Grade 11**

Taking time for interaction with the Creator and Redeemer makes learning valuable and transformative.

By mercy and truth iniquity is purged: and by the fear of the LORD men depart from evil.   Proverbs 16:6 KJV

Throughout my life, I failed to see how school could be transformative. I always thought it was just a requirement for society. My public-school experience was most indicative to that. I decided to try homeschooling shortly after moving into a farmhouse. Still my opinion on school was the same, and without any inner purpose, it was done. Math, previously my favorite class, became increasingly confusing and extremely frustrating! I needed transformation, so for my first year of high school, I started Griggs International Academy after an interview with them. I liked the order and simplicity of it. But my story stayed the same until I met the principal and Bible teacher. She was an experienced teacher as well as inspiration as to what we call, "Griggs Life." Through many months of theology assignments, discussion-based assessments, and personal artistic projects in the Bible I class (required for the first year of any newcomer) and in every other class, I finally saw what education truly was about, development through the exposure and exercise of new ideas being valuable to the mind and body. Griggs International Academy as a whole enabled education to be a joyful experience instead of a dull one. I was not being carelessly pushed into education, but rather, was being inspired and transformed into this service. In the years spent involved with Griggs, I also ended up quitting forever the distractions and habits that are usually formed with "freedom."

Griggs also enabled and encouraged more personal time with the Creator and Redeemer. Teaching eternal lessons with time and experience in God's Word is quite convenient with my daily schedule. I am grateful for the transformation God has made in my life.

Shane W.   **Grade 10**

> **God is not unjust; he will not forget your work and the love you have shown him as you have helped his people and continue to help them.**   Hebrews 6:10 NIV

I am the type of person who will always help others and put their needs first. Last year, I wanted to help everyone and it got pretty exhausting, especially since some people saw that and took advantage of me. I would put their needs before my own and I took being helpful and serving to an unhealthy level. This physically and emotionally drained me, and my immune system slowly started getting worse and worse, among other things. I would easily get sick. At first, they were just little colds that I got over easily. But then about two weeks ago, I got some form of strep throat. I've had this a couple times before when I was younger and treated it with antibiotics for ten days and it did the trick. I went to the doctor and they prescribed antibiotics. I started taking them and everyday my strep throat just kept getting worse. So, I started taking a double dosage of antibiotics thinking that would help, but it just kept getting worse. Finally, ten days passed and antibiotics hadn't helped at all. At this point, my throat was so inflamed and swollen that I could barely breathe, swallow, or speak and it started spreading down my throat. My mom was very scared and we didn't know what to do.

At this time, my mom started attending a medical missionary school where medical missionaries from all over the world came to Serbia for six months to teach others. She expressed her concern about my illness to them and they told her

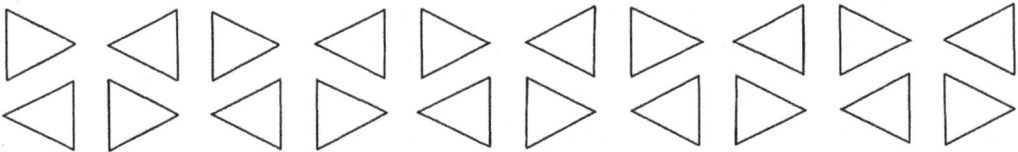

that I could come to their institute and be their patient so that they can treat me. I packed some essentials and left. I arrived on a Sunday. They would give me treatments everyday to help build my immune system back up. There were girls that were constantly taking care of me and there for me. Everyday, I did many treatments, was on a juice cleanse, and took many healing essential oils. Little by little, my strep throat got better. By the next Sunday, I was well. The spreading had stopped, the white spots had disappeared, and the inflammation had gone down. It was a nice change to not only be taken care of but shown love. You could really tell that these people had love in their hearts, loved serving, and wanted the best for me. This experience really touched me and made me think about becoming a medical missionary because I love helping others as well.

You could really tell that these people had love in their hearts, and loved serving, and wanted the best for me. This experience really touched me and made me think about becoming a medical missionary because I love helping others as well.

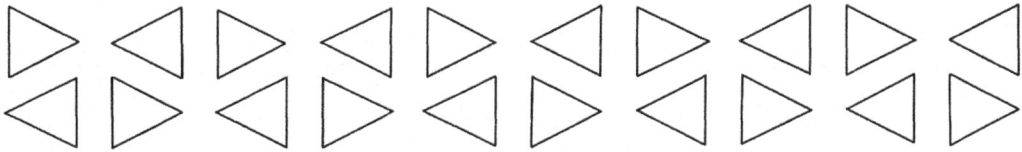

Anastasia M.   **Grade 12**

Therefore, encourage one another and build one another up, just as you also are doing. 1 Thessalonians 5:11 (NASB2020)

As an aspiring content creator, I like making videos and other content to publish online. It's a rewarding hobby and business to me. Despite the great opportunities, rewards, and enjoyment, it can definitely be a grind. Sometimes it is hard to be motivated. I can get overwhelmed and discouraged. It is a time consuming hustle and hobby.

I have gotten a lot of inspiration and encouragement over the past few years. I have family members and friends who watch, subscribe/follow, comment, and like my content. Even people I'm not that close to sometimes engage with my work. That's not all. There are some who consistently support my efforts. Some talk to me about it and ask how it's going. People I've never met thank me, support me, and encourage me. There's more! I've had someone ask me about my hobby and then sent an inspiring call to action for me which meant a lot to me.

If the things I've mentioned aren't cool or inspiring enough,

*Ask God to help you be more like Him
so you can be an inspiration to others*

listen to this. Early this year, I was messaging a good friend of mine and the topic of my content creating came up. She then said that someone she knew thought highly of my videos. I can tell you that the passing comment meant the world to me. It literally made my day. It encouraged, excited, and inspired me. It in fact carried over to a degree to the following days and I still think about it from time to time. What seems so simple has meant a lot to me.

The inspiration, support, and encouragement I've received from many people really motivates me. The following aren't new ideas of mine – in fact you've probably read, watched, and listened about them. The Bible talks about it too. Therefore, be an inspiration and encouragement to others. Show your support and care. It could be in words or actions. It often is pretty easy and doesn't take much time, but it means a lot, as I can attest. Take that a step further and do it from a spiritual aspect. With God's help, you can be an inspiration by your actions, example, and word. Love others and follow His Word. Be a witness.

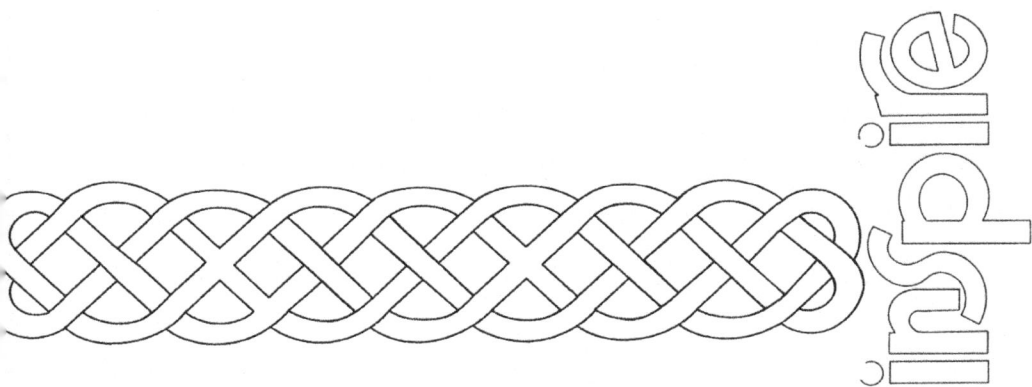

inspire

Jadon K.   Grade 12

Let your life shine before others, so that they may see your good works and give glory to your Father who is in Heaven.

When the war broke out in Ukraine in 2021 my dad, working for ADRA - the Adventist humanitarian organization, was sent to the borders of that country to coordinate the relief response to those fleeing.

For as long as I can remember, my family has been surrounded by missions. For us, serving is our way of giving back to God. My sister and I had the opportunity to fly in after our dad and there we witnessed the suffering of mothers and children left with nothing but a few bags. We got to spend quality time with them, help them use all the resources available, and reassure them that they would be taken care of.

It was such an eye-opening experience that left all the volunteers in tears and feeling more gratitude for what God has given them than ever. It made us all understand the importance of community and acts of service. It was a blessing to all of us present. It is one more experience I have been blessed to add to my collection of priceless memories of service in action.

Serving, whether it be in your community or someplace around the world, should be the greatest joy in our lives. Being a blessing to others, using our gifts for good as the mission God set out for us...What better way to give back to God?

Elsa B.   **Grade 11**

For God has said, "I will never fail you. I will never abandon you.

Hebrews 13:5 ESV

In my town we have an annual county fair. It's typical to find a friend to pair up with to go on all the rides, play games, and have fun with, so you don't have to be stuck with your parents. When I was in eighth grade, and I decided to pair up with one of my closest friends. After I got to the fair with my family and met up with my friend, I realized she had invited another friend as well. I didn't mind this other friend tagging along, but I wasn't super close with them. My friend had also committed to staying with her sibling at the fair, so the group was different than what I had planned on. We had fun throughout the day, trying to pair up as much as possible, until we got to the Ferris wheel. Neither I, nor the other friend wanted to go on the Ferris wheel with the younger sibling. The other girl and I got into a cart, and my friend and her sibling got into another. After a few minutes, my friend spotted her ex-boyfriend. The one condition she really had at the fair was to stay with her little sibling. She wasn't bound to us, though she had said she'd hang out with us. However, when she saw the boy, she got off the ride and left our friend and me in the cart, up in the air, as well as her sibling and went to hang out with her ex. We eventually got off the ride, but she was nowhere to be seen.

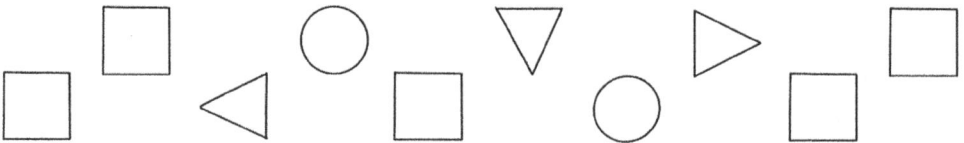

If the other person can't change their ways, change yours. Reflect God in the hopes that they'll have him as a friend too.

Later, we found her. She had joined up with her ex and a couple of other friends, deciding to hang out with them instead of coming back to hang out with us. That group was foul-mouthed, and not the best crowd for me to be around. Instead of acting angrily and storming off, I quietly left and went back to my parents for the rest of the evening.

One lesson I learned from this experience is that no matter how much faith or trust you have in a person, they're still human. They still might turn on you, or break a promise, or hurt you. They might ditch you for someone else. You can't change that. But no matter what, no matter how many times people hurt you, just know that God is always going to be there for you. Hebrews 13:5 says, "For God has said, 'I will never fail you. I will never abandon you.'" Keep this in mind as you go through life. Know that God will always fulfill his promises, God will always be there for you, even if you can't see Him, and most of all, God loves you. If the other person can't change their ways, change yours- reflect God in the hopes that they'll have him as a friend too.

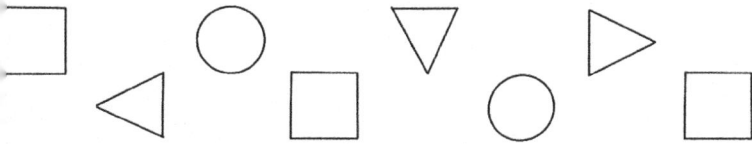

Ashley S.   **Grade 10**

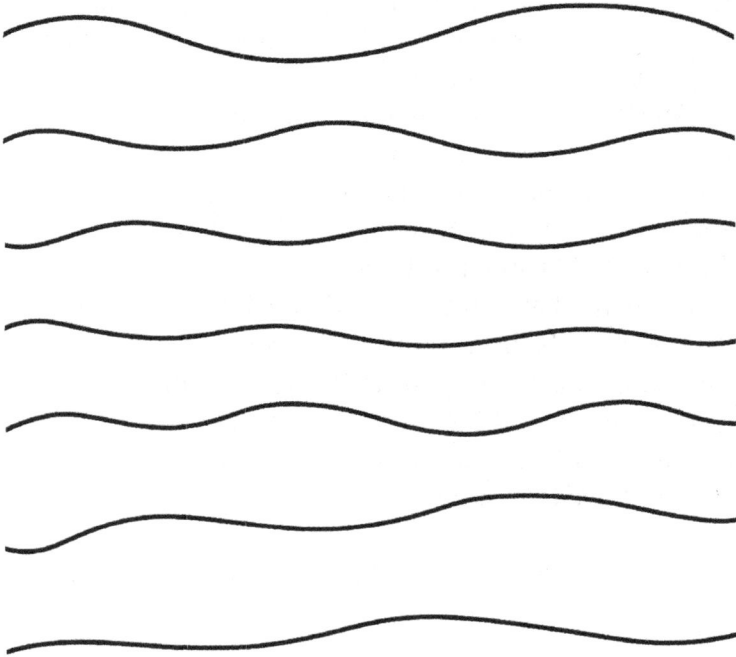

*Strengthen your relationship with Christ, and
He can use your change to inspire others.*

And the prayer offered in faith will make the sick person well; the Lord will raise them up. If they have sinned, they will be forgiven.

James 5:15 NIV

Sometimes as Christians we get into a routine with God. We will pray in the morning, before meals, before bed, and have devotions every day. We will go to church, read our Bibles, and repeat this over and over. Having a schedule to spend time with God is amazing, and we should make sure that we always have time to spend with Him, but that doesn't mean we have to stay the same. I used to think that once you have a great relationship with God, nothing really changes. God fits into your routine, and you live out your life, but that way of thinking and living has changed for me.

Over the past few years, my mother has been dealing with autoimmune and other diseases. It got to the point where we were out of options, and nothing seemed to be getting better. It was in this moment that we realized that we should seek God for help more in our lives. We decided to ask our church for an annointing. This was not only to ask God to hewlp my mom to get better, but also to forgive her sins. James 5:15 talks about annointing and what it means, "And the prayer offered in faith will make the sick person well; the Lord will raise them up. If they have sinned, they will be forgiven."

After her annointing, my mom started to feel better. But not only that, she changed. She started to pray more and spend more time with God. She was happier and talked about Jesus and his promises more regularly. This transformation in her inspired me. You never know who will notice your change. It helped me realize that our relationship with God can always get better, and that others truly notice Jesus in our characters. Strengthen your relationship with Christ, and He can use your change to inspire others in the same way my mom has inspired me.

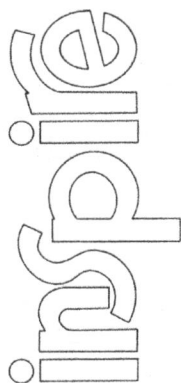

Shayla R.   **Grade 11**

Loving God transforms us for the better, that
we may in turn transform others

And now these three remain: faith, hope and love. But the greatest of these is love.   1 Corinthians 13:13 NIV

I remember asking my father a simple, yet subsequently deep question I'm sure often crosses most minds: "How do we get ourselves to do what is right?" I was given a short answer to end our short-lived conversation: "Love God." My father's response seemed so vague and cryptic. What did one have to do with the other? After some further thought, in an attempt to decipher his statement, I reached some solid conclusions.

Though doing what is right may seem complex, it is as simple as developing a good relationship with God that in turn becomes love for Him who first loved us (1 John 4:19). Loving God transforms us. In our love for God, we are led by our conscience to please Him as we would anyone we truly love. This leads us to doing what's right. Jesus says in John 14:15, "If you love me, keep my commands." Doing what is right begins with learning to love God. Our love for Him then compels us to willingly do that which is right in His eyes. By living such a life, not only are we transformed, but we in turn transform everyone around us through the fruits of our love for God.

Love is mentioned approximately six hundred times in the Bible, depending on your translation. These mentions cannot be by mere coincidence. This amount of repetition surely signals towards love's immense importance and significance. It prompts us toward the first step to becoming the person God wants us to be. Loving God transforms us for the better, that we in turn may transform others alike.

I was on YouTube one day and an ad interrupted my video. Naturally, I was about to skip it, but it intrigued me. It was about a young woman sharing her testimony. She spoke about going through a challenging time in her life and being very frustrated with God. At that moment, she began to pray. But, being tired of her rehearsed prayers, she openly explained her anger towards her situation and told God that she was frustrated that he was allowing these things to happen in her life. She even expressed that she didn't really want to talk to Him in the first place! After her prayer, she felt a peace wash over her that wasn't like any other feeling she had ever experienced. She said that God then softly spoke to her and said that he wanted to see her fully express herself to him, even if it wasn't flattering words. This hit me like a ton of bricks. I realized that my prayers were rehearsed and scripted and it wasn't even on purpose. However, it never occurred to me that I was being dishonest with God about my feelings. If I was angry, I wouldn't tell him. I would simply thank him for my blessings and ask for forgiveness and grace. My true feelings were never aired. I often found myself with bottled

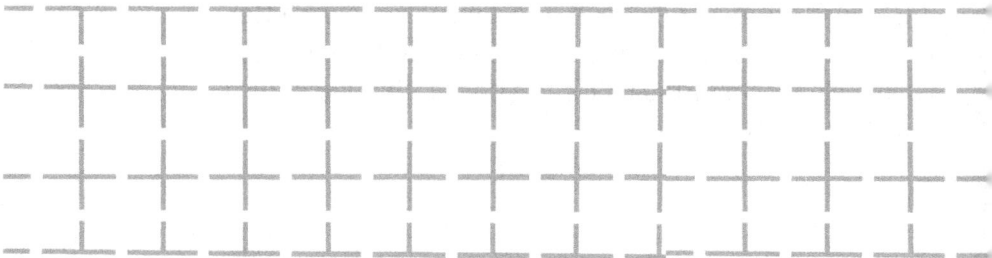

Give God all of your burdens that hang over your head.

feelings that I had nowhere to release. Like anyone in a relationship, we want people to be honest with us. God does too. He wants to know exactly what's on our minds, the good, the bad, and the ugly. He doesn't care if we don't always agree with him, because we wouldn't be human if we did. Instead, he wants us to speak our thoughts just the way they are. In fact, he treasures them!

The longest book of the Bible is an honest and intimate communication between God and his child (David). Sometimes David fully trusted God's plans and didn't question them, while other times he didn't understand what God was doing and it frustrated him. He even got upset from time to time. But either way, he always told God about it. It's not that God doesn't know what's truly on our hearts, but he wants to see if we trust him enough with our raw, unfiltered emotions. My favorite reason is that He really cares about how we feel. So why not give it a shot?

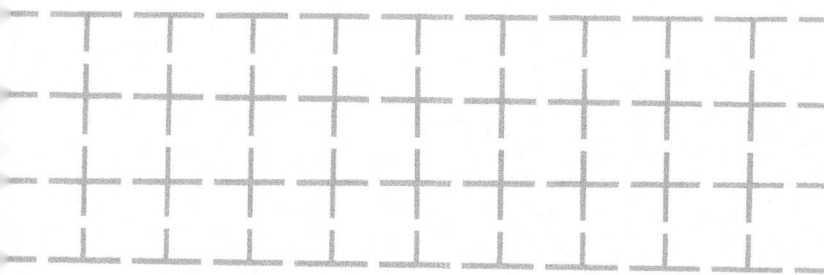

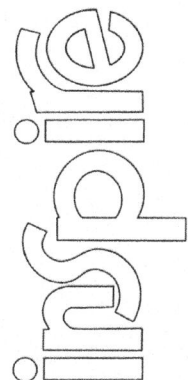

inspire

Avianna C.   **Grade 10**

Ever since I was a child, I have been enthralled by dinosaurs. But it has only been in the last few years that I realized I wanted to make dinosaurs a career choice.

About three years ago, I was given the chance to return to one of my most favorite spots in the whole world: Camp Cretaceous. Every year, a group from Southwestern Adventist University goes out to Wyoming to dig out dinosaur bones. They bring a group of people from all over the world to take a class about the bones for college or high school credit. For three years, I was able to take that class.

I like to think that there is a time when every person must make the decision "Am I going to believe what I've always been taught? Or am I going to search and find the truth for myself?" I had been struggling with this thought for a while. Finally, after "wrestling with God" I told Him: "If You will allow me to meet two kids my age, who have the same level of fanaticism about dinosaurs as I do, I will trust that You know what You are doing."
So, I went off to the dig, ignorant of what I had just gotten myself into. I showed up, helped set the tents up, and helped unload the vans. Then the first Monday, while I was walking out to the quarries,

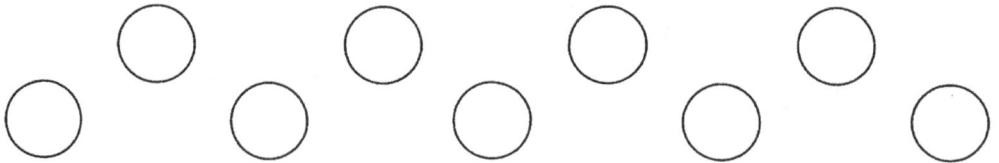

the place where we find the bones, I noticed that there were two guys, about my age, going on and on about dinosaurs. What do you think happened?

Well, I now have two friends who I talk with regularly about new dinosaur discoveries, and who also want to become paleontologists. Do you think I was just a little shaken that day? King Belshazzar's knees had nothing on me! (See Daniel 5:6). To this day, I will never forget how I became transformed by God, there in the midst of the fossils.

You may not know what you want to do with your life, but I guarantee that if you ask God to direct you, He will show you what His plan is for you. In a way, I was INSPIRED by the dig, to be TRANSFORMED by God, so that I could SERVE Him by telling others about the evidence I see, there in the dust.

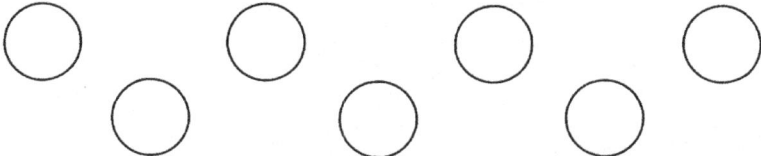

Morgan W.   **Grade 11**

As the clock struck four o'clock, I was glad to realize that the long day of school was finally over. Clearing my books off of my desk, I peered out the window. Outside was dark and dismal, the bare trees and chilly breeze signifying that the Fall was now turning into Winter.

With this kind of weather, a warm, delicious meal would really hit the spot, I thought to myself. Being reminded of how hungry I actually was, I quickly finished tidying up and ran downstairs.

"Hey Mom!" I called out. "What's for dinner?"

"Divini, I don't know yet, but it looks like it won't be much", she replied.

"Oh", I said disappointingly. "But I'm so hungry. We've only had two bananas for breakfast and very little food for lunch.

"I know," Mom sympathized. "But you know things have been rough, but God will provide. How about you help me look around and we'll see what we can find".
I turned to the pantry, searching for ingredients for dinner, but barely found anything.

This had been our daily routine for the past couple weeks. When Dad lost his job, money was short and at every meal, we were never sure what our next one would be.

Suddenly, in the midst of this stress, there was a knock at

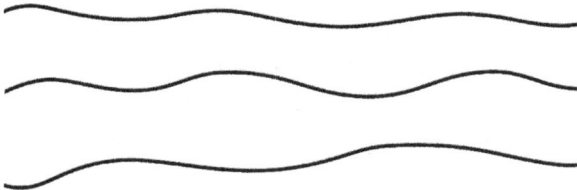

Be willing and ready to lend a hand of service - you never know how much of an impact your act of kindness may have

the door. Seeing that it was Ms. Jackie*, a good friend of ours, Mom answered it. After greeting each other, Mom noticed Ms. Jackie's car parked in our driveway, the trunk overflowing with groceries. Ms. Jackie smiled, turned around, and started to unload all the groceries onto our doorstep.

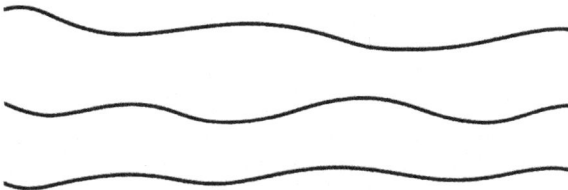

"Wait, are all these supplies for us?" Mom exclaimed.
"How did you know that we were desperately in need?"

"I didn't know," Ms. Jackie replied. "But I was impressed by God to bring groceries over, and so, I did. I hope they are of help."

After everything was unpacked, the reality of this miracle really hit us. Just minutes ago, we had nothing, and now, a sea of groceries sat right before our eyes.

God had provided in an extraordinary way! This experience inspired me to strengthen my faith in God and never doubt His miracle-working power. In addition, this lady's small act of service towards my family inspired me to be more intentional about serving others – you never know how big of an impact your act of kindness may have.

Divini-Loryn B.   **Grade 10**

_____

_____

_____

_____

_____

_____

_____

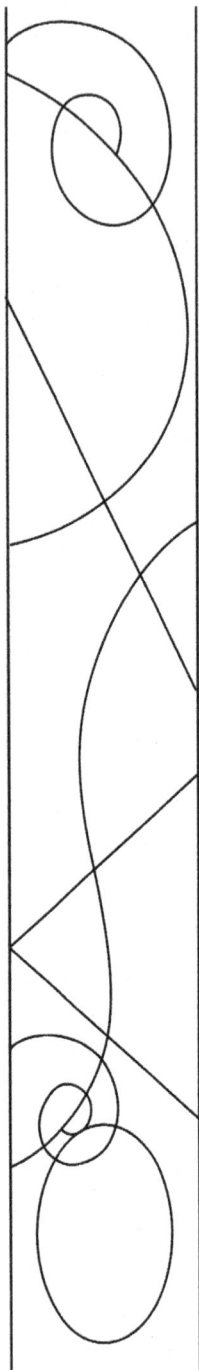

Find a person with a strong radar for good people.
You will learn a lot from them.

But it is the spirit in man, the breath of the Almighty, that makes him understand. Job 32:8 NIV

Think about one person in your life who has greatly inspired you. Some will say their parents, or a friend, or a famous person. The person I want to tell you about is my mentor. On Wednesday November 3, 2021, I got a text message. The text was short, just asking me to meet them on Zoom. At first, I panicked. The meeting ended up with this person asking me to join the student task-force where we help the administration of the school generate ideas for student involvement and success. I was shocked to even be on the radar for such a position. It turns out that the person I met with on Zoom had a sixth sense about people. They see the good in someone and know when a person has big places to go.

I took inspiration from this because I also want to see the good in people. I want a sixth sense to be able to see all the potential in those around me. The task-force position has helped me grow so much. I feel more confident about having a voice, and I am less afraid to go against the tide. I have grown because I was seen by someone and they put their faith in me.

Think about your person of inspiration. Do they see the good in you? How you can learn to look for the good in people and always have your radar turned on so that you just might be that inspiration to someone else. My mentor inspired me to push myself and to step outside of my comfort zone so I could become a better person.

Yuliya H.   **Grade 12**

From my experience, friends are essential to make it through the rough times in life. During the early stages of COVID-19, my middle school switched to virtual learning. Similar to many, I was disconnected from in-person interactions with people. This disconnection made me feel lonely. Then, I remembered I had friends.

When I called on some of these so-called "friends," all they did was make me feel more alone and miserable. However, when I called on two of my closest friends, they encouraged me. They helped me feel better about virtual learning by helping me see the bright side of it. We even did Bible studies, virtually, once a week. We shared Bible verses and talked about Bible stories it reminded us of. We also had conversations about how our week was going and how we felt. To this day, we encourage each other and pray for each other. We do this because we want to become better friends. But most importantly, we want to build a character that is Godly.

There are many Biblical friendships that relate to this, but I believe the friendship between David and Jonathan relates best to this story. The Bible says in 1 Samuel 20:14-17, 42 that David and Jonathan swore an oath of friendship that would extend

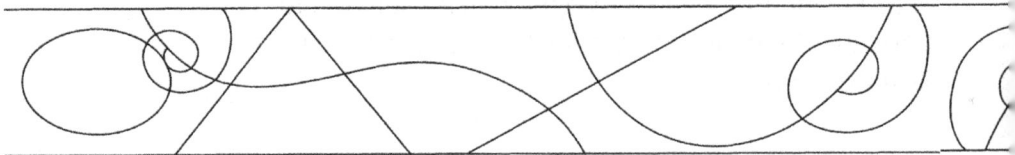

Ask God to instill a reliable character in you.

One who has unreliable friends soon comes to ruin, but there is a friend who sticks closer than a brother. Proverbs 18:24 NIV

through their generations. Even though Jonathan's father, Saul, was impolite toward David, they still managed to form a friendship that ultimately saved David's life. The Bible also says in 2 Samuel 9 that after Jonathan's death, David kept his promise and took care of Jonathan's lame son, Mephibosheth.

These are the types of friends we should want in our lives. I believe God is willing to give you friends who are reliable and will encourage you when you need it. Also, God is willing to give you friends who are Godly. I pray that you will ask God for friends that embody a Godly character and reliability. In addition, I challenge you to ask God to instill that character in you. So that you will be the friend that embodies the character of God.

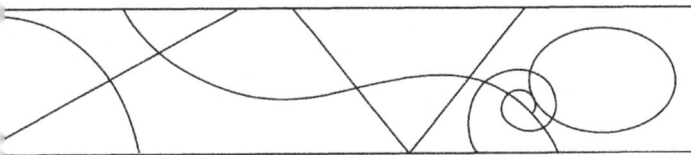

transform

Michaela C. **Grade 9**

_____

_____

_____

_____

_____

_____

_____

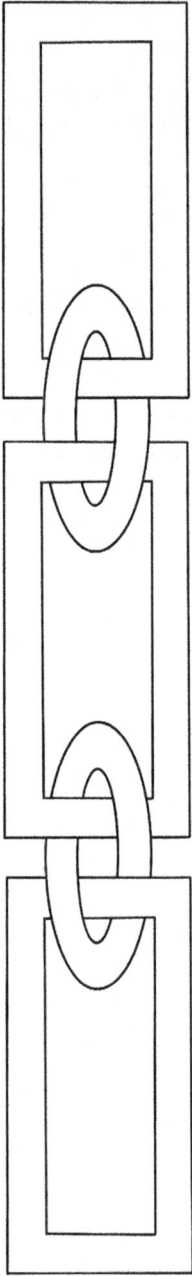

Your life is way better with God involved.

I am the vine; you are the branches. If you remain in me and I in you, you will bear much fruit; apart from me you can do nothing.

John 15:5 NIV

On September 25 2021, at the age of 13, I made the biggest decision of my life: I got baptized. I wasn't sure if it was the right decision at the time, but I knew that it was what I wanted. When I was baptized, I felt like I finally belonged to something. Now, almost one year later, I know that it was the right decision. Giving my life to Jesus was one of the best decisions that I ever made. It made me feel closer to God and it has helped me a lot in my life. The experience changed my life and I am so grateful for it. One thing that made me feel closer to God before I got baptized was preaching. I have been preaching since I was three years old! I preached about giving your life to God and it was ever so helpful to so many people. Maybe three months after getting baptized, I decided that I wanted to start a youth bible study on Tuesdays. Starting this group made some huge changes for me. I started connecting with the youth in my church and kept the group going. Once doing so, I started focusing a lot more on God and grew my relationship with Him. Ironically, that became my downfall. As I kept trying to make room for God my schoolwork was getting out of hand and I blamed God for it, even though it was my fault. I wasn't setting my priorities straight. Eventually, continuing with my schoolwork and going towards my first year of high school, I realized that I needed a balance of God and school. Now, every morning I wake up and read my bible for five to ten minutes. Then, I watch a portion of my recorded sermons to get the day started. I now realize that life is better with God in it. You can also live life better with God in it.

Aleeiah H.   **Grade 9**

Have you ever experienced fear that paralyzed you to the point where you froze and did not know how to react? About 10 years ago, I had an experience that shocked me to the core. As a teacher for the Georgia-Cumberland Conference at the time, we were given the opportunity to take a day off each year for a Spiritual Renewal experience at Cohutta Springs Conference Center. This particular year, I decided to take my day in April. I readied myself with some inspiring podcasts, my devotional, and my Bible then hopped in my car for the 2 hour journey to Crandall, Georgia. Upon my arrival, I decided to get unpacked and change into some comfortable clothes.

Cohutta Springs is situated in a valley on a lake so it is surrounded by gorgeous mountains. Around the perimeter of the lake is a walking path. I thought it would be a good idea to go for a prayer walk before sunset. Keep in mind, I was walking in the forest just as winter was coming to an end. As I was walking, I would periodically stop and talk to Jesus. I felt His presence in a very real

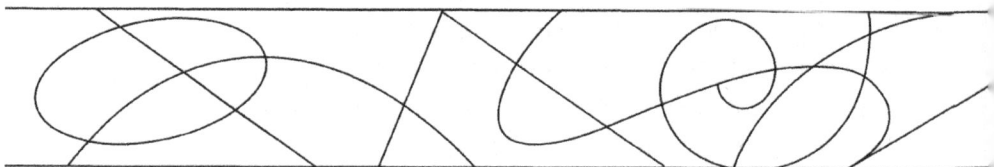

In the midst of fear, rest assured that God is with you and will help you.

way along this walk. About three fourths of the way around the lake, I heard a very strange grunting sound that I had never heard before. So, I turned in the direction of the sound. It was a very large, very hungry black bear. I froze in fear. I had three options: Go down the mountain to the lake, Go up the mountain in the direction of the bear, or continue on the path away from the bear. I was afraid to move and did not know what to do so I just froze. At this moment, I prayed intensely and asked Jesus to help me. The Holy Spirit told me to walk backward very slowly away from the bear. So, I did.

Once the bear was out of my sight, I ran full speed back to the conference center. My heart was racing. But, my heart was full. This experience solidified to me that Jesus is always with me... in times of happiness, sadness, fear, distress and even confusion. We can always turn to Him for comfort and He will give us peace.

transform

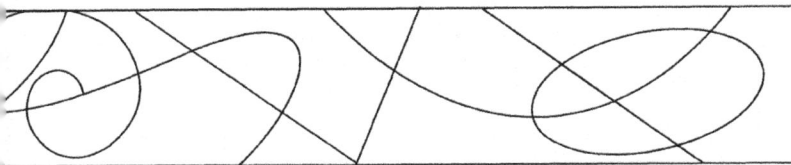

Tammy B. **Staff**

_____

_____

_____

_____

_____

_____

_____

Don't let the worries of this life be the obstacle that keeps you from obtaining the very best.

Still others, like seed sown among thorns, hear the word; but the worries of this life, the deceitfulness of wealth and the desires for other things come in and choke the word, making it unfruitful.

Mark 4:18-19 NIV

A long time ago, almost forty years ago, I started working at summer camp. Our director was Ron Scott. He is a wise man who loves Jesus. He started the summer with a review of the previous summer. It was an introductory worship for the staff. The previous summer was plagued with a "peeping Tom." It was very frightening to the girl's cabin counselors. The men on the staff determined to put a stop to this very real threat. They spent many nights patrolling the woods around the girl's cabin, but never actually caught the "peeping Tom" in spite of more visits to our camp (He was arrested near the end of the summer by the Sheriff's department.). This issue took all the time, energy, and effort of the staff.

When the summer was over, Ron Scott realized that they, as a staff, had been less successful at sharing Jesus with the campers than he had hoped. The time and energy focused on this major problem lessened the time and energy they could put into the campers.

In life, we have very real distractions. Don't take your eyes off the important elements of school. You will not have another year in the same grade, with the same classmates again.

Jesus warns us about this difficulty in our own lives. In Mark 4:1-20, He tells us about the sower who goes out to sow. (You can also find the parable in Matthew 13 and Luke 8) I want to focus on Mark 4, verses 18-19, shown above. Don't let the worries of this life be the obstacle that keeps you from obtaining the very best. God has given talents and entrusted you to develop them.

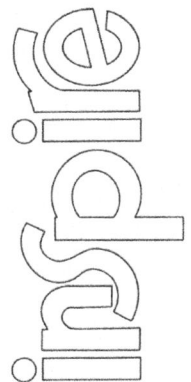

Harley P.   **Staff**

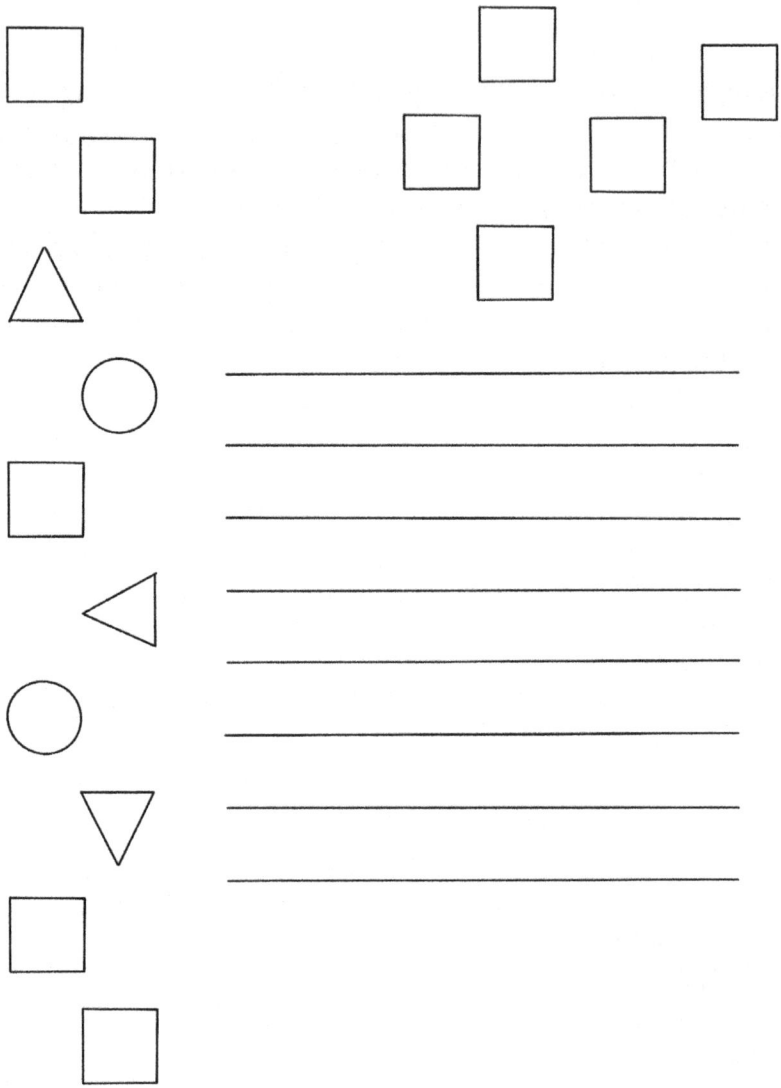

Focus on important things, capturing only the positives.

For now we see in a mirror dimly, but then face to face. Now I know in part; then I shall know fully, even as I have been fully known.   Corinthians 13:12 NIV

Photography brings out the best or worst in people as it captures monumental events and creates memories in all forms. As a picture is viewed, feelings are recreated or interpreted differently than when first taken, giving new meanings to life. Does this "change" mean you are not a good photographer? Absolutely not! Holly Carpenter was told "Everyone can be a photographer." You are probably wondering, "What does this mean?" Well, simply put, the interpretation of a photograph is unique to each person. There is not wrong or right way unless trying to reflect a specific technique or story. There is no way to fully capture what you are seeing or thinking when taking a photograph which means all can be considered an amateur photographer.

You can take the ultimate photograph in a botanical garden that will not adequately describe its beauty. Your opinions and views of said photograph would be valid as it is your interpretation. However, photographs only give an overview or slight inkling of their true meanings.

The same goes for our Heavenly Father. Though the Bible is an important and powerful tool, it vaguely depicts how heaven will be. The text above seems to validate this idea.

As you continue in your studies, continue to take shots at bettering yourself, keeping in mind that everyone learns differently, and outcomes will differ. Focus on the important things, capturing only the positives after reaching a goal or not. At the end of this life, you will have a portfolio of only positive memories as these will negate any undesirable experiences not suitable for the kingdom.

Lamar N.   **Staff**

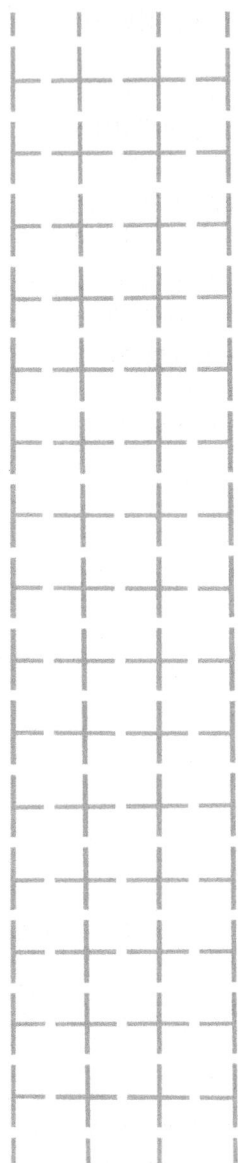

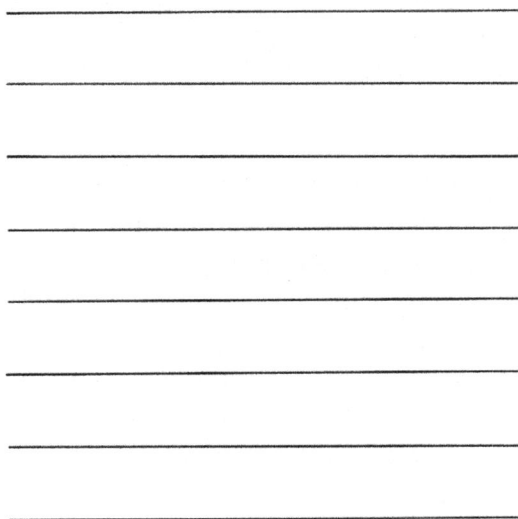

We can't be the underdog if we have Jesus on our side.

In this world you will have trouble. But take Heart! I have overcome the world

John 16:33 NIV

I remember the first time I realized I had gotten the David and Goliath story all wrong. I had always been taught that it was the classic underdog story. In a way it is, but not at all like how I had thought.

When Saul tries to discourage David from fighting, David replies saying, "When a lion or a bear came and took a sheep from the flock, I went out after it and attacked it, and rescued the sheep from it's mouth; and when it rose up against me, I grabbed it by its mane and struck and killed it. Your servant has killed both the lion and the bear." (1 Samuel 17:34-36)

The sling was a deadly weapon in the hands of someone trained. It is estimated that some soldiers were accurate enough that they aimed for not the head, but a specific part of it. They could launch these stones at over 60mph. In Judges 20, we see that the tribe of Benjamin (Saul's tribe) specialized in this form of warfare. Verse 16 says there was an elite group of left-handed warriors who could aim their rock at a piece of hair and not miss.

David had spent his life in a country known for their abilities in war, and he had long been honing his skills against lions and bears. And to top it all off, this man was God's anointed who relentlessly pursues God's heart of love and justice for His people.

Oh, it's an underdog story alright. Goliath doesn't stand a chance. Goliath was undoubtedly a formidable challenge in many ways. Yet when faced with someone walking alongside Jesus, the outcome had already been decided. In Jesus' final moments with His disciples, He tells them of the challenges they will soon face. He doesn't wish them luck or tell them it will be easy. Read the verse above with His message to the disciples.

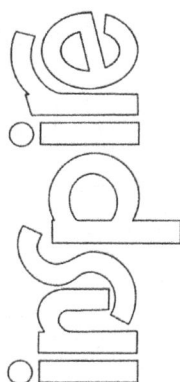

Ben K.   **Staff**

_____

_____

_____

_____

_____

_____

_____

_____

> **Show yourself in all respects to be a model of good works, and in your teaching show integrity, dignity.**
>
> Titus 2:7 NIV

There are several times throughout the year that we take time to celebrate different people groups within our world community. While it is difficult to showcase every heritage, we love to recognize diversity within our Griggs community. We have students from over 50 different countries and our diversity is reason to celebrate.

Let me tell you about a high achieving woman from the Hispanic community. She is born with Mexican heritage and grew up in California. Have you hard of the NASA astronaut Dr. Ellen Ochoa? She received NASA's Distinguished Service Medal, NASA's highest recognition. In 1993, she was part of a mission that went into space on Shuttle Discovery. She is the first Hispanic woman on a space mission, and she took a part of daily routine with her. She practiced her flute in space! Believe it or not, she played Vivaldi on the space shuttle. Would you keep up your music practicing if you were in space? She is also a co-inventor for three patented technologies, and she helps with raising awareness on childhood cancer. What an amazing role model!

Ochoa has a strong passion for education and career choices. When asked about her influence on young people, she said "Being an astronaut is a wonderful career. I feel very privileged. But what I really hope for young people is that they find a career they're passionate about, something that's challenging and worthwhile." She is known for telling students to Reach for the Stars!"

https://www.nasa.gov/centers/johnson/about/people/orgs/bios/ochoa.html

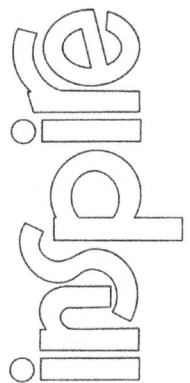

La Ronda F.   **Staff**

I visited a farm with my family in Novembet. The farmhand was gracious enough to let my kids go into the coop and pick some freshly laid eggs. (And the chickens were gracious enough to hand them over!) On the way home one of my kids said, "Wouldn't it be fun to see if they'll hatch?"

At first, the teacher in me was thrilled and immediately started planning with them, making lists of the things we needed and researching how long it would take for them to hatch. And then the mom in me stepped in and realized that if this project didn't have the happy ending my children expected (hatched eggs), they would be horribly disappointed. But I was too far into the plan to change course.

I started prepping the kids for the chance that maybe the eggs weren't viable and they wouldn't hatch. Every day they would put a check mark on their calendar as they counted down to "hatch day." And every day I would remind them, "Remember guys, this is an experiment. Remember the eggs might not be viable." Still, we waited and wondered if there was anything happening inside those little eggs. Until the day finally came: Hatch day. And just like that, a week shy of Christmas, like some

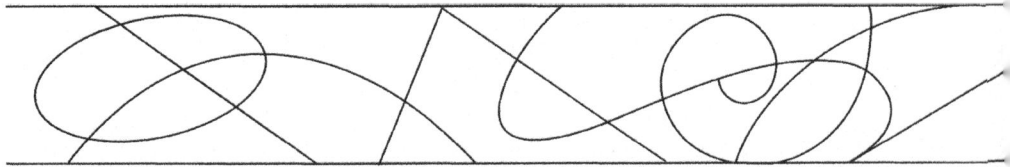

Though things may look uncertain, God is working. Have hope.

But seek first the kingdom of God and His righteousness, and everything else will be added unto you.

Matthew 6:33 NIV

kind of divine Christmas miracle, the mysterious eggs began to hatch! I couldn't believe it. Hour after hour, one by one, each chick chipped away at their shell until not one, but ALL FOUR eggs hatched and four health ADORABLE little chicks emerged.

That night as I read the story of the birth of Jesus, the most important Christams miracle, my kids quietly cuddled their chicks as they listened. For me, it was a huge epiphany. I just thought to myself as I read, "That's how it was with Jesus. The people all probably thought

the same thing I did . . . "maybe He'll come, we should watch and wait." "Nah, He won't come. But will He? . . . When""

Until the day came. And no one knew it would. And no one expected it. And then, just like that, Jesus was born.

I don't know what you may be waiting for in your life, or if there is a prayer that God has yet to answer for you. Remember, things may look uncertain, but God is always working. Have hope.

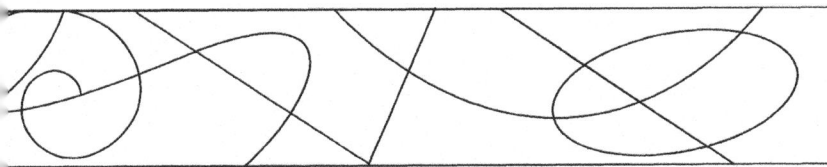

Luz G.   Staff

Made in the USA
Las Vegas, NV
27 November 2023

81630046R00036